Quotes o...
Anc...
Interpretations, A
Words Of Wisdom
Collection Book

Edited by
D. Brewer

Copyright © 2020 D. Brewer
First published in January 2020 by
Lulu.com

Distributed by Lulu.com

All names, characters, businesses, events and incidents are either the products of the author's imagination or used in a fictitious manner. Any resemblance to actual persons, living or dead, or actual events is purely coincidental.

ISBN-13: 978-0-244-55054-7

First Edition

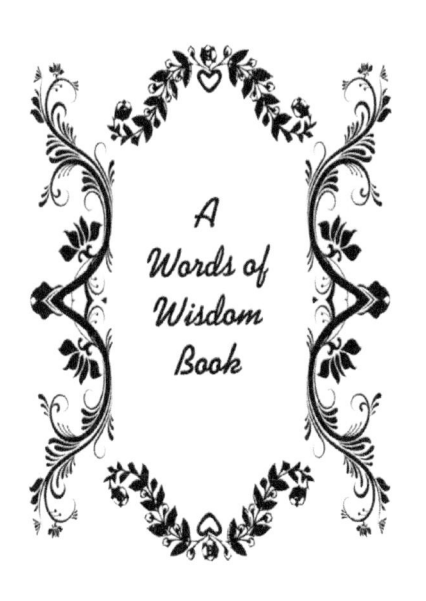

A Words of Wisdom Book

Quotes Of Confucius

Quote:

If you shoot for the stars and hit the moon, it's ok. But you've got to shoot for something. A lot of people don't even shoot.

Meaning:

You should always aim for your highest goals, and do not be despondent if you don't quite reach them. It is better to at least try, than not to try at all.

If you don't quite reach your goal, at least you will still have achieved more than when you started.

Furthermore, if you achieve something different from your intended goal, then you have still been successful.

Unfortunately many people are lacking in ambition, and for them, any kind of success becomes impossible.

Quote:

If you hate a person, then you're defeated by them.

Meaning:

You achieve nothing useful through hating someone. The emotion of hate is strong and more harmful to yourself than the person you hate. It can consume you.

Furthermore, if you apply hate to a person, then you are allowing your thoughts to give the idea of them attention. If they have your attention, then they are successfully distracting you from more worthy contemplation.

If a person is not worthy of your attention or has wronged you, then better to forget them than hate them. In this way, you are maintaining your self-respect.

Quote:

The man who moves a mountain begins by carrying away small stones.

Meaning:

This quote points out that a seemingly impossible task, one that appears too huge to manage, can still be achieved by beginning with small steps. You should not be discouraged by the size of the task.

If you want to change something great, then small changes will be a start. They will make a difference, however small, and will be steps in the right direction.

Quote:

The noble-minded are calm and steady. Little people are forever fussing and fretting.

Meaning:

This points out that wise people remain calm and unflustered at all times, even in difficult situations. "Fussing and fretting' is not a wise reaction. It has no benefit, and little can be achieved.

Being 'calm and steady' allows for clear thinking and planning so that a difficult situation can be considered, understood, and drawn to a successful conclusion.

'Fussing and 'fretting' leads to confusion and an inability to prioritise or plan efficiently.

Quote:

If your plan is for one year, then plant rice. If your plan is for ten years, plant trees. If your plan is for one hundred years, educate children.

Meaning:

For a short term plan to succeed, then you only need to make provision for that short length of time. Therefore you should only invest in a short term idea. For example, planting rice will feed people for a year. The grain will only take a year to grow and will provide more grain.

For a medium term plan, you have to consider how you will be able to maintain your plan for an increased length of time. You must invest in a medium term growth idea. For example, trees will take longer to grow, but they will also last longer, and will provide fruit every year.

But in the long term, this quote highlights the importance of education. A long-term plan can only succeed if the people inheriting the plan can properly understand it in order to continue it and improve upon it.

When your consider your goal, you must always contemplate the length of time, and the type of investment required to achieve the goal, and then factor this into your plan of action.

Quote:

The superior man acts before he speaks, and afterwards speaks according to his action.

Meaning:

This implies that a wise person will use their own actions and experience to exemplify what they have to say, rather than speak on a subject on which they have no previous experience. In doing so, they will gain the respect of the people they are speaking with, leading or instructing.

Also, by acting first, they will already know the result of those actions. They will also have gained an understanding of the most efficient way to carry out that action. It would be foolish to instruct someone on a deed that may not even be achievable.

Even if the actions of the wise person did not result in success, then it is still a benefit to those he speaks with, so that they do not commit the same mistakes.

Quote:

Silence is a true friend who never betrays.

Meaning:

If you have a thought or knowledge of something, about which you do not want other people to know, then the only true friend you can rely on is silence. In other words, do not tell anyone. Then this knowledge cannot be passed on.

Silence can also be beneficial in situations of conflict and argument. Remaining silent can empower you, leaving the opponent with no one to argue with.

Silence also gives you time to properly consider your argument before expressing it. It will stop you from reacting inappropriately with emotional kneejerk reactions instead of considered. analytical responses.

Quote:

The man who asks a question is a fool for a minute. The man who does not ask is a fool for life.

Meaning:

The word fool, merely means ignorance. We are all ignorant of everything we do not yet know. Therefore, if you ask a question, you display an ignorance, only until you have the answer. You will be able to learn and expand your knowledge by admitting an ignorance.

Asking the question may make you feel briefly foolish because others will already know the answer. It is even harder when they already expect you to know. But this feeling will pass quickly.

It is far more foolish not to ask, because then you will always be ignorant and you will never learn.

Quote:

When anger rises, think of the consequences.

Meaning:

This is telling us not to react instinctively, but to give thought to our reactions. It tells us to understand the consequences of reacting in anger before we react, and asks us to evaluate whether the angry reaction is actually worth the consequences, which it seldom is.

You have a choice over your responses. You can choose not to be angry.

Quote:

Things that are done, it is needless to speak about. Things that are past, it is needless to blame.

Meaning:

This is a two part quote. The first part explains that speaking about a bad thing in the past has no benefit.

The second part, similarly, explains that there is no benefit in blaming anyone for a bad thing that is in the past. There is no value to be gained from bringing up the past and laying blame.

If you do not recount bad things of the past to others, then they are less likely to mimic or repeat those bad actions, or proportion blame onto figures of the past.

Remonstrating about past deeds takes time and energy that could be diverted towards more virtuous and more beneficial pursuits.

Quote:

The man who thinks he can and the man who thinks he can't are both right.

Meaning:

This clever quote implies that a person's success lays very much in their mindset.

They are much more likely to achieve a goal if they think they can and they believe in their own abilities to achieve it. They are willing to keep trying until they reach success.

But if they think they can't, then they probably won't, even though it is the same goal, as they are far more likely to allow self-doubt, insecurity and fear of failing influence their confidence, leading to self-sabotage of the project through giving up.

Quote:

He who learns but does not think is lost. He who thinks but does not learn is in great danger.

Meaning:

This is another two part quote. It suggests that firstly, you must think about what you are learning, or there will be no understanding or benefit from the subject. You may attempt to partake in that subject, but you will be lost in any action or conversation about it. You will not know what to do, and you will not understand what is being said.

Secondly, if you think, but do not learn, i.e., you fail to research the subject you are thinking about, then you might indeed be placing yourself in danger through your own ignorance. A wise person will always think and learn. And if you think you can partake in an action without first finding out about how to do it, then danger is definitely likely.

In both situations, you are also failing yourself. That is the danger, because you are not giving yourself a chance to learn and expand your knowledge.

Quote:

When you see a good person, think of becoming like him. When you see someone not so good, reflect on your own weak points.

Meaning:

Be observant of those around you. Imitating the positive attributes of another person is admirable self-improvement.

When you see someone displaying not such good attributes, this is a reminder and an opportunity to look in the mirror to identify your own similar weaknesses with an aim for changing yourself for the better.

Quote:

The man who chases two rabbits, catches neither.

Meaning:

This explains the futility of reckless greed. If you want for too much, you will spread yourself too thinly and be unable to give your goals the necessary attention required, and therefore you will end up with nothing.

Only attempt one goal at a time, so that you can give it your full focus and energy. Your productivity and efficiency will be greater as a result. One successful outcome is better than two failures.

What is more, when you chase and catch just one rabbit, i.e., you achieve success in one goal, you will benefit from the increased enthusiasm and the drive to go on to achieve another success with your next goal.

Quote:

People with virtue must speak out. People who speak are not all virtuous.

Meaning:

In this quote, Confucius is urging wise and good people to speak up and let themselves be heard above others. It explains that there are voices from people who do not necessarily speak truth, and therefore, honest voices must become louder, in order to guide people towards truth.

It also suggests that we should be aware that what many people say may not be true, and that there are those among us, possibly even figures of authority, who do not lead honest lives.

It is for us to use wisdom to recognise the virtuous among the many, to avoid being fooled by the untrue voices of those who do not lead the kind of 'good' life that they would have us believe.

Quote:

It is better to light one small candle than to curse the darkness.

Meaning:

In any difficult situation, it is better to do some good, however small, than to simply complain about it. Complaining achieves nothing and benefits no one.

Even just one small step towards solving a problem, as in one small candle to create light, is better than doing nothing.

The word darkness, can also be a metaphor for ignorance or evil.

In the case of ignorance, it is better to try educate yourself and others than to allow a population to remain in ignorance of true facts.

Even if just one person manages to learn something.

In the case of evil, it is better to do one small good deed, than to let evil flourish unchallenged.

If you do not at least try, in all of these examples, then you have no right to complain about the circumstances.

Quote:

A man who has committed a mistake and does not correct it is committing another mistake.

Meaning:

If a person makes a mistake and has the opportunity of righting it, then they should do so. By not righting it, a second distinct mistake is made. It is not just a continuation of the first mistake.

If you make a mistake, then you must take responsibility for it. You can reflect upon the mistake, learn from it and make progress through its correction.

Quote:

Wheresoever you go, go with all your heart.

Meaning:

This lovely quote tells you to put your heart and soul into everything you do and everywhere you go. Your own personal experience will benefit greatly and your enthusiasm will radiate from you, positively affecting everyone around you. Then you will lead a full and satisfying life.

Quote:

It does not matter how slowly you go so long as you do not stop.

Meaning:

With whatever project or goal you are working on, if you feel it is moving too slowly, you should not be despondent. You must continue with your goals and never give up.

If you give up, you will waste the progress you have made so far, and you will never tend towards achievement.

Quote:

Our greatest glory is not in never failing, but in rising every time we fall.

Meaning:

While working towards your goals, do not worry about setbacks. With every setback, you must get up and continue.

A setback provides an opportunity for self-reflection, learning and experience. The failures of the past are an education for the future.

Getting back up is admirable and shows courage and strength of character. Use your past failings to make you stronger and more wise. You have furthered your knowledge and increased your chances of future success.

Therefore it is far better to rise after a fall than to stop. Never give up. You must persevere through the journey of your life towards your goals.

Quote:

Life is really simple, but men insist on making it complicated.

Meaning:

This is absolutely true. After all, we don't really need much more than just food, water, warmth, clothing and shelter. Everything else is a human complication, caused by expectations, overthinking, over-ambition, and the need for approval.

Remove these complications, and life not only becomes simpler, but also easier and happier.

Quote:

Choose a job you love and you will never have to work a day in your life.

Meaning:

If you have a dead end job that you work at to pay the bills, just so you can get to the weekend to enjoy yourself before returning to the dreaded Monday again, then life becomes hard, like a treadmill.

But if you follow your passion, then your work becomes a joy. Bills are still paid, and every day feels like the weekend.

Quote:

Never do to others what you would not like them to do to you.

Meaning:

This basic maxim of treating others as you would like to be treated, may be simple, but it is so important. All may be well now, but when you have problems, you may need your friends, acquaintances or colleagues.

So always be there for them when they need you, so that they may return the favour when the tables are turned.

Quote:

Death and life have their determined appointments; riches and honours depend upon heaven.

Meaning:

The day you are born, and the day you die, are unchangeable certainties, out of our control, regardless of how many honours you achieve in your lifetime, or how many riches you possess.

True riches and honours may only be rewarded after death in heaven. All other riches and honours are meaningless as they hold no value or benefit to yourself when you are dead.

Another interpretation of this quote is that between the day you're are born and the day you die, if you lead a good life, you will be rewarded in your lifetime with riches and honours, determined by heaven.

Quote:

Ability will never catch up with the demand for it.

Meaning:

This suggests that you can always improve your ability in whatever skill you choose.

It is impossible to achieve a level of complete total saturated ability as there will always be room for improvement.

The demand for ability will always exist because humans will always want to achieve more, to explore more, and to create and invent more.

Quote:

The superior man, when resting in safety, does not forget that danger may come.

Meaning:

This means that you should never become complacent. Do not become smug or indulge in arrogance, as situations can change at any time, often when you least expect it.

When times are quiet, and life seems easy, be prudent about your circumstances. Be careful not to take relationships or finances or any other aspects of life for granted.

Quote:

If a man be under the influence of anger his conduct will not be correct.

Meaning:

If you react while you are angry, you are likely to make a mistake.

Reactions should be dealt with calmly. When in a calm state of mind, you can consider your reaction and make sure it is appropriate and beneficial.

Similarly, your behaviour will be adversely affected when you are in a state of anger. You may do or say things that you may later regret, leading to unintentionally hurting those around you who you would least want to hurt.

Taking the time out to recognise your emotional state, and taking steps to avoid reacting angrily is essential.

Quote:

Faced with what is right, to leave it undone shows a lack of courage.

Meaning:

You must always do what is right, regardless of how difficult it is.

If you choose not to do the right thing, simply because it is the easier course of action, or choose to do nothing, then this is cowardice.

Quote:

Forget injuries, never forget kindnesses.

Meaning:

When you have been wronged by someone, forget about it. Do not retaliate or plan revenge. This will not achieve anything good for either you or the person who hurt you.

Conversely, when someone is kind to you, and has done right by you, always remember it and remember them. Show gratitude towards them. Be the same to them, and should you need them again, they will be happy to be there.

Quote:

Hold faithfulness and sincerity as first principles. Then no friends would not be like yourself.

Meaning:

If you are always faithful and sincere, you will attract friends of the same virtues.

Friends who are neither faithful nor sincere are not true friends.

Quote:

In archery we have something like the way of the superior man. When the archer misses the centre of the target, he turns round and seeks for the cause of his failure in himself.

Meaning:

This metaphor relates to achievement. When you do not achieve a planned goal, do not look for others to blame. Similarly, do not look to blame and chastise yourself. Look to yourself and try to understand the cause.

This is an opportunity for self-reflection and personal growth. It is a time when you can learn and understand more about yourself.

Find out what you could change in yourself and your actions to help you reach your goal the next time.

Quote:

It is easy to hate and it is difficult to love. This is how the whole scheme of things works. All good things are difficult to achieve; and bad things are very easy to get.

Meaning:

You have to work hard to be a good person. Cheating, taking short cuts and doing things the easy way may lead you to not such good ends.

In every event to which you partake, you should do your best, however hard it might appear.

Furthermore, it is hard to love someone who may have wronged you, but you should try. Hating them is easier, but will do you no good. It is a destructive emotion that causes anguish and stops you from being able to move on with your life. You should become the better person and practice forgiveness. Through this action you will come to feel a comforting sense of closure and a satisfying confidence in knowing you are doing the right thing.

Quote:

Look at the means which a man employs, consider his motives, observe his pleasures. A man simply cannot conceal himself.

Meaning:

Through observation and study of a person's behaviour, you will find the truth about that person. Consider how he does something, why he does it, and what he gains from it.

No matter how much they try to hide it, the truth will always come out in the end.

Quote:

Only the wisest and stupidest of men never change.

Meaning:

This clever little quote explains how a true wise person knows that they have no need to change. They are in control and aware of the consequences of their actions. They are educated and able to presume the success of their intended goals.

A stupid person has much need to change, they are just too ignorant and stupid to realise what necessary changes are needed.

Quote:

The superior man is all-embracing and not partial. The inferior man is partial and not all-embracing.

Meaning:

It is wise to entertain, learn, understand and respect all ideas and cultures presented to you. With the backing of a wide general knowledge, clever sensible decisions can be made.

If you shun some of them, then your general knowledge will be lacking, your life experience will be diminished and you can miss out on valuable information leading to an inability to make complete well thought out decisions.

Quote

The superior man is aware of righteousness, the inferior man is aware of advantage.

Meaning:

It is better to do the right thing, than the thing that will give you a greater advantage over others, whether financially or in status.

Looking ahead at the right course of action is to take a path towards a successful conclusion for all. Looking only for personal gain will serve you in the short term, but at the expense of others.

Doing the right thing will bring you respect.

Quote:

What the superior man seeks is in himself; what the small man seeks is in others.

Meaning:

It is wise to look at what you can change and improve about yourself in order to achieve a goal. (For example, educating oneself and self-reflection).

An unwise person will be looking to blame others, or expect others to change and help them achieve their own goal. In this case, they would be unlikely to achieve it.

Quote:

Without feelings of respect, what is there to distinguish men from beasts?

Meaning:

The complicated feelings we experience are what make us human. Our respect for each other underpins our social relationships, and our respect, in general, for everything in the world, is what separates us from animals, who do not possess such sophisticated feelings.

If we choose to show no respect, then we are behaving as animals.

Quote:

The cautious seldom err.

Meaning:

This has three similar interpretations.

Firstly, it is wise to take care to consider all factors before making a decision in order to avoid making a mistake.

Secondly, by showing caution, rather than rushing a decision, errors are less likely.

Thirdly, if you choose not to take any chances, then mistakes cannot be made.

Quote:

In all things success depends on previous preparation, and without such previous preparation there is sure to be failure.

Meaning:

When you have a goal in mind, it is wise to make a plan for how you will achieve this goal. Preparation is key to success. For example, if your goal is to pass an exam, then you must prepare by revising. If your plan is to gain a work promotion, then you must hard work towards it. If your goal is to win a race, then you must practice for it. In all of these, without the essential preparation, you are unlikely to reach your goal.

Quote:

Better a diamond with a flaw than a pebble without.

Meaning:

It is good to be the best you can be in your own truly unique way. We are all unique, just like each diamond. Diamonds are also rare. A truly unique person is rare and will not be afraid to have imperfections.

You may have different styles, beliefs and ideas. That is better than trying to look and behave like everyone else, just to conform, covering up your flaws, so that you become as common and uninteresting as a pebble.

Quote:

When you have faults, do not fear to abandon them.

Meaning:

A wise person will recognise their weaknesses and will not be afraid of learning and self-improvement with an aim to change themselves to overcome their weaknesses.

They will not be afraid to admit their faults when they come to light, with a view to letting them go.

Quote:

I do not want a friend who smiles when I smile, who weeps when I weep, for my shadow in the pool can do better than that.

Meaning:

A friend who merely imitates your mood, mimics your actions and agrees with your every thought and word is not one who can genuinely benefit you.

A true friend can be relied upon to question your decisions and encourage you to towards doing what is right. They will be there with you at the darkest times, to offer hope and reason, and at the best of times, to offer praise and respect.

Quote:

To practice five things under all circumstances constitutes perfect virtue; these five are gravity, generosity of soul, sincerity, earnestness, and kindness.

Meaning:

The five virtues listed in this quote should together, always be part of your every thought process, decision, action and communication. If all these are used at all times, then you can achieve greatly.

Confucius went on to explain the reasoning behind the five virtues:

- If you are grave, you will not be treated with disrespect.

- If you are generous, you will win all.
- If you are sincere, people will have trust in you.
- If you are earnest, you will accomplish much.
- If you are kind, this will enable you to employ the services of others.

Quote:

The superior man is satisfied and composed; the mean man is always full of distress.

Meaning:

A wise person is virtuous and works for the benefit of all. As such, they are at peace with themselves.

A mean person works merely for their own self-interest and personal gain. Therefore they are perpetually caught up in fearful and vicious competition with their peers, with greed at their base, leading to a nervous state of distrust within the mean man.

Quote:

They must often change who would be constant in happiness or wisdom.

Meaning:

To be constantly happy and wise, you must be prepared to and even embrace change.

Clinging to the past will not ensure continued happiness. The past will fade and change will always inevitably happen around us as a natural form of evolution. We must be able to recognise the changes, and understand how to change within ourselves to maintain a happy state.

Quote:

With coarse rice to eat, with water to drink, and my bended arm for a pillow – I have still joy in the midst of these things. Riches and honours acquired by unrighteousness are to me as a floating cloud.

Meaning:

We only need the basic things in life to be happy. When you have very little, you can still find happiness.

If you attain wealth and reward through immoral means, they will have little true value or substance, similar to 'a floating cloud', and will not bring you true happiness.

Quote:

Consideration for others is the basis of a good life, a good society.

Meaning:

A wise person will always show respect, kindness and consideration to their fellow human and as a result, will be thought of as virtuous.

If all people within a collective show these qualities towards each other, then society as a whole becomes virtuous. Such actions will also perpetuate a good society as the children will acquire and demonstrate the same qualities from their parents and peers.

Quote:

I want you to be everything that's you, deep at the centre of your being.

Meaning:

Within this quote, you are being asked to truly look deep inside yourself. Recognise who you really are, away from the influences of those around you.

When you can lose the ideals placed upon you and absorbed by you from others, and see who you really are, then you can understand and learn to become your true self.

To be complete and fulfilled, you must understand your own values, desires, wants and needs and then embrace these as a testament to your own individuality and uniqueness.

When you achieve all this, then you can be wholly you, untainted by the ideals of others.

Quote:

Study the past, if you would define the future.

Meaning:

A wise person will use lessons learned from the past, when planning for the future. They will consider past failings and mistakes, and investigate and understand them, in order to determine a better future, assured by the non-repetition of previous errors.

This applies on a micro personal scale through self-reflection, as well as on a macro societal, national and even international scale through the observation of history.

Quote:

There are three things which the superior man guards against. In youth ... lust. When he is strong ... quarrelsomeness. When he is old ... covetousness.

Meaning:

A wise man will guard against lust while young, as many a man has been led astray through impetuous youthful infatuation. But lust may also be applied to wanting unnecessary superficial riches.

Later on, he must guard against being quarrelsome when he is strong. Arguing and fighting will encourage a disrespect among his peers, and will fracture the bonds of human friendship. Relationships must be nurtured and maintained for mutual benefit.

As an old man, he must guard against being greedy, jealous and wanting the material possessions or honours of others. If he is wise, he will be satisfied with what he owns and what he has achieved through his life. He will be calm and steady, self-assured and secure in the knowledge that he has all he needs and there is no requirement for being covetous.

Quote:

When you are labouring for others let it be with the same zeal as if it were for yourself.

Meaning:

It is important to put in as much enthusiasm and effort in your work for other people, as you would in your own. Even if they are the ones who benefit from the rewards of your efforts. You will still appreciate the satisfaction of good work. You will also gain the respect of others.

Not putting in the same amount of effort will not benefit you and will lead to personal dissatisfaction.

Quote:

The superior man is distressed by the limitations of his ability; he is not distressed by the fact that men do not recognize the ability that he has.

Meaning:

When a wise person finds their skills are not good enough to accomplish a task, it will be difficult to come to terms with. Such a person will be irritated, and motivated to try to improve on them through learning and practice.

However, when they have particularly good skills, they do not require to be praised or applauded for them. They do not perform their skills to gain reward or honours or to show others how great they are.

Instead, they apply their skills to perform actions to quietly benefit others, not themselves, without the expectation of appreciation.

Quote:

He who speaks without modesty will find it difficult to make his words good.

Meaning:

It is wise to remain humble in every sentence you utter. People rarely truly respect words of the self-proud.

A wise person will not crow about their own abilities. They will look outward and speak of the good in others. They will choose words carefully, and with thought and consideration.

Quote:

Ignorance is the night of the mind, but a night without moon and star.

Meaning:

A night sky without a moon or a star is empty and dark. There is nothing to guide you in your pursuits, or to draw knowledge from.

A night sky with no moon or stars has no information for you to consider. Such is the state of an ignorant mind.

Quote:

Real knowledge is to know the extent of one's ignorance.

Meaning:

It is untrue for any person to state that they are not ignorant in any way. We are all largely ignorant when you consider the vastness of the universe.

A wise person will recognise their ignorance and admit its enormity, and strive for a life of learning and understanding.

Quote:

The object of the superior man is truth.

Meaning:

A wise person will always aim to be virtuous. They will strive to learn and understand life and the universe around them. They will not be motivated by greed for wealth or recognition and honours.

Quote:

Is virtue a thing remote? I wish to be virtuous, and lo! Virtue is at hand.

Meaning:

This quote clearly explains how simple it is to be virtuous.

It is not a difficult concept to understand. Neither is it a skill to be learned, or an art requiring practice. It is simply a decision, and the desire to follow through that decision.

Quote:

The firm, the enduring, the simple, and the modest are near to virtue.

Meaning:

These are the traits that people need to possess and maintain to tend towards leading a truly virtuous life. To be steadfast, to endure, to be simple and humble takes calm thought and consideration before every word and action. Therefore to remain virtuous, a wise person must persist in these traits.

Quote:

The man of virtue makes the difficulty to be overcome his first interest; success only comes later.

Meaning:

This quote continues the theme that a wise person does not work for riches and honours. The objective of their effort is to overcome whatever obstacle they are facing.

The task at hand is more important than the rewards and recognition of the success of that task.

Quote:

Virtue is not left to stand alone. He who practices it will have neighbours.

Meaning:

A person who is always true will always have friends. A virtuous person will always be there for a friend, and in turn, will always have respect and appreciative friends there for them, even though this is not their objective.

A less than virtuous person risks ostracizing and jeopardising relationships with those close to them through distrust and lack of respect.

Quote:

Everything has its beauty, but not everyone sees it.

Meaning:

To see beauty, even in the most unlikely places, you must take time to consider the intricacies of Mother Nature and marvel at the detail in all things.

Only when you consider the elaborate complexity of every possible entity, can you begin to understand and recognise the beauty in everything.

Unfortunately, many people will not take the time to see this.

Quote:

Before you embark on a journey of revenge, dig two graves.

Meaning:

Revenge is a damaging reaction. A person with an obsession for revenge is following an unvirtuous path. Revenge will stoke an anger within themselves and cause them to become plagued with torment.

Revenge does not recompense a wrong doing. It does not change the past. It consumes a person, changing their moral attitude, leading to actions from which no good can come forth.

Quote:

I hear and I forget. I see and I remember. I do and I understand.

Meaning:

One interpretation of this quote is that in education, a person does not learn effectively by merely being spoken to. When a skill is demonstrated, they will remember it, but to truly understand it, they need to actually have a go themselves.

A second interpretation suggests that you never truly understand another person's perspective until you are placed in their shoes, experiencing the same as them.

Quote:

Your life is what your thoughts make it.

Meaning:

You have control over your destiny. No one but you has control over your thoughts, and from these come your ideas and actions, and through these you design your life. Therefore, your thoughts are the starting blocks of how you choose to live your life.

Quote:

The journey with a thousand miles begins with one step.

Meaning:

No matter how long your journey, or how hard your task appears, you must make a start, however little. Without starting, no progress is even possible, nor any potential for success or even partial success.

Every venture will have a starting point from where an objective can be approached. Do not let the size of the venture discourage you.

Quote:

You are what you think.

Meaning:

Your thoughts determine your words and deeds. Your chosen words and deeds define how you are perceived by others. Therefore, take care to always think virtuous thoughts.

Let your thoughts lead you to become wise, humble, considerate and kind.

Quote:

Looking at small advantages prevents great affairs from being accomplished.

Meaning:

This implies that you must always look at the greater picture. When you have a plan, you must work towards the final outcome.

If you only aim for the small rewards that can be achieved along the way, you will be distracted and delayed from the ultimate plan, and risk straying from it.

Quote:

All people are the same; only their habits differ.

Meaning:

We are all the same species. We are all human. It is our cultures and beliefs that differ. We are born the same, and our peers influence and educate us as we grow, encouraging habits that differentiate cultures.

Even at a micro societal scale, a young child is influenced differently by their immediate close relations from a neighbours child, bringing forth different habits among two neighbouring children in the same society.

Quote:

Learn avidly. Question it repeatedly. Analyse it carefully. Then put what you have learned into practice intelligently.

Meaning:

A wise person will always learn as much as possible about a specific topic. And rather than merely absorb it, you should always query what you have learned. Test its validity for better understanding and truth. And then when putting it into practice, apply your own common sense, rather than blindly following instructions.

Quote:

We have two lives. The second begins when we realise we only have one.

Meaning:

A young person will rarely recognise their mortality. They will feel like nothing can harm them and they will live for ever. As a result, their behaviour may be reckless.

Alternatively, they may not be living their best life, or living life to the full.

When we realise we only live once, a new phase of life begins. That is when we start to take care of ourselves and make the most of our lives, fulfilling our dreams and achieving our goals.

Becoming aware of our mortality can encourage us to achieve our best, to be remembered for the good things we have done after we are gone.

Quote:

If you are the smartest person in the room, then you are in the wrong room.

Meaning:

A wise person will understand that they will benefit greatest from people smarter than themselves. The process of learning should always be an objective.

However, be wary of thinking that you are the smartest person in the room. It is very likely that this is only your opinion, and quite possibly wrong. Much can be learnt from other people when you realise that on some topics, they are actually the smarter ones.

Furthermore, displaying a belief that you are the smartest person in the room will encourage disrespect from your peers. You should always be respectful of others, and realise that there are many levels on which they are smarter than you.

Quote:

Act with kindness, but do not expect gratitude.

Meaning:

Expecting gratitude for your kind actions is a self-centred reaction. We should complete our good deeds without a thought to ourselves.

Our aim should be purely to benefit the recipient of the kind action, not to receive recognition or honour.

Quote:

Worry not that no one knows you; seek to be worth knowing.

Meaning:

The fact that you are unknown in your field is irrelevant and should not be a cause for concern. It is more important to do your best.

Set your goals high and work your hardest to tend towards achieving them. In doing so, you will earn respect from your peers and they will come to value your efforts. Then, without intention, you will be worth knowing.

Quote:

When it is obvious that the goals cannot be reached, don't adjust the goals, adjust the action steps.

Meaning:

When you realise that you are not going to be able to achieve a task, you should think about what you could do differently. What actions could you take that will enable you to achieve it?

Do not simply accept an easier task, and do not give up. Consider a different approach to the problem, even if it means going back to the beginning of the original idea, back to the drawing board.

Quote:

The essence of knowledge is having it to use it.

Meaning:

The essence, is the basis, or concept, or intrinsic nature of the word.

To achieve anything at all, a person must strive to gain knowledge first.

To have knowledge, is to have the ability and skills required to achieve anything. Nothing can be done in life without the knowledge to do it. But then, you need knowledge of what you need to know. Such is the intrinsic nature of the word.

Quote:

One joy dispels a hundred cares.

Meaning:

The importance of joy, or happiness is such, that a moment of joy can enable a person to forget their many woes. The feeling of happiness greatly outweighs feelings of sadness and distress when delivered in the same quantity.

Therefore, give joy to the people you meet. Exude happiness and love, and the shadows of heartache will dissipate.

Quote:

I slept and dreamt life is beauty. I woke and found life is duty.

Meaning:

A beautiful carefree life is a wonderful ideal, but not a realistic one. Life comes with responsibilities, no matter what walk of life you come from.

Caring for those around you, being the best person you can be, striving for knowledge, expecting nothing, serving others before yourself, earning your place in life through practicing virtue… these are your duties.

Quote:

Don't complain about the snow on your neighbour's roof when your own doorstep is unclean.

Meaning:

You should always be tolerant. Consider your own flaws before you complain about another's. Question yourself first. Are you really that much better? Criticising a person will encourage resentment, self-doubt and hurt in that person.

Quote:

A lion chased me up a tree and I greatly enjoyed the view from the top.

Meaning:

From every difficult situation, an advantage can be found or gained. When being pushed hard in a task, the value in the effort becomes apparent when you reach the top and feel the sense of achievement.

Another interpretation of this quote is that staying calm and on top of a problem will enable you to enjoy the process of solving it.

Quote:

Be not ashamed of mistakes and thus make them crimes.

Meaning:

We all make mistakes. When an error has occurred, you should not cover it up, or be embarrassed. To cover up a mistake or withhold knowledge of it from others to avoid taking responsibility for it is devious. To be embarrassed by a mistake is self-hurting.

Accepting the mistake, and more importantly, learning from it, turns the error into a beneficial experience.

Quote:

The superior man is modest in his speech, but exceeds in his actions.

Meaning:

The old adage, actions speak louder than words can be considered another form of this.

A wise person will always strive to complete any task to the absolute best of his/her ability, but will not crow about these actions for personal benefit, recognition or admiration.

Furthermore, they will do more in their actions than they say. They will excel in their deeds, but not exclaim it.

Quote;

Be strict with yourself but least reproachful of others and complaint is kept afar.

Meaning:

You should always expect nothing less than the best from yourself. Learn the most you can, strive your hardest, and remain virtuous.

But you should not expect others to be the same. Furthermore, you should not complain when others are not behaving in the same manner. Then you will find that they will have little to complain about you.

Quote:

Roads were made for journeys, not destinations.

Meaning:

The 'road' is a metaphor for striving for achievement. The final achievement of the task is not the purpose of the 'road'.

The true purpose is the learning, practice and action that leads towards the final 'destination', or successful achievement.

Our lives contain many such roads along which we must journey. But we should properly and completely value the experience of the journey itself.

Quote:

No matter how busy you may think you are, you must find time for reading, or surrender yourself to self-chosen ignorance.

Meaning:

The value of reading to gain knowledge from others, or from the past is immense and as such, essential. With knowledge comes ideas, ability, skill and potential achievement.

If you choose not to read, then you will learn little. That is a poor choice from which you will gain no benefit.

Quote:

Think of tomorrow. The past can't be mended.

Meaning:

Whatever has occurred in the past is an event that cannot be changed, so there is no benefit in wishing it were different or lamenting over it. The future is in your hands and there to be created by yourself. You have control over what happens in the future, so that is where you should move your thoughts and considerations to. Your experience of the past can be used to benefit your future, so looking forward is where your focus should be.

Quote:

Respect yourself and others will respect you.

Meaning:

Self-respect is an internal necessity for confidence and personal growth.

Recognising your own true value will naturally attract respect from others without deliberately attempting to gain it.

Quote:

To be wronged is nothing unless you continue to remember it.

Meaning:

A wise person will not dwell on something that has hurt them in the past. If they did, then it would continue to adversely affect them.

Therefore, it is better to move on, moving forward with your life, and the memory of that hurt will fade and dissipate away to nothing.

Quote:

By nature, men are nearly alike. By practice, they get to be wide apart.

Meaning:

All people are born similar, with no moral opinion or belief. But as they grow, they are influenced by their peers in society, leading to differences of varying degrees among cultures, religions and nations of people.

Quote:

Learn as if you were not reaching your goal and as though you were scared of missing it.

Meaning:

Imagine you have a goal to achieve. Then imagine you are not going to achieve it. Use the fear of not reaching it to fuel your enthusiasm, drive and energy towards learning and striving for success.

Quote:

Never contract friendship with a man that is not better than thyself.

Meaning:

A wise person will always try to associate themselves with those who are better than themselves to gain insight and influence from them.

Through befriending them they will be able to recognise their strengths and imitate their virtues with an aim to bettering themselves.

Quote:

He who knows all the answers has not been asked all the questions.

Meaning:

It is arrogant, even foolish, for a person to assume they know everything about a specific subject. In truth, they are likely to know less, as they are unaware that more questions exist on the subject.

Therefore, when searching for knowledge, do not necessarily ask the one who declares they are the expert.

Quote:

Those who cannot forgive others break the bridge over which they themselves must pass.

Meaning:

In order to be able to move on in life after a person has been wronged, they must find a way to forgive the person who has wronged them.

In doing so, they will also give that person the opportunity, motivation and encouragement to forgive themselves. Otherwise, they will both be unable to move forward in life.

Practicing forgiveness enables both the wronged person and the wrong doer to lay the past to rest.

Dwelling on the past and perpetuating blame can cause both the wronged person and the wrong doer to sink into the waters of depression instead of traversing the bridge of healing.

Quote:

They who know the truth are not equal to those who love it, and they who love it are not equal to those who delight in it.

Meaning:

Knowing the truth, loving it and delighting in it are three separate ideas with an ascending level of virtue.

To know the truth is to understand what is right and virtuous. But to understand it is not as good as loving it.

To love the truth is to be bound by a need to live by its ideals, fulfilling a life of virtue. But this still is not as good as delighting in it.

To delight in truth is to know it, love it, and be abundantly joyous in having truth become part of your very nature, exuding truth from your very centre, so that nothing else can tarnish its brilliance as it shines through your human existence.

Quote:

The superior man thinks always of virtue. The common man thinks of comfort.

Meaning:

It is wise to live the most virtuous life.

When faced with a decision, choose the one that will do the most good for others, not the one that will be motivated by a selfish desire for your own comfort or benefit.

Truth, patience and remaining humble should always be at the forefront of your mind when considering your options.

Quote:

Education breeds confidence. Confidence breeds hope. Hope breeds peace.

Meaning:

When you have a deep knowledge about something, you become self-assured and confident in that subject. A good, broad education within a society enables the people to feel accomplished and capable. It also give them an understanding of the importance of peace and tolerance.

That confidence allows them to feel a hope for the future because they have a sense of well-being, and the ability to achieve, which leads to motivation and optimism.

With this positive effect, a peaceful society will exist, one where the people will co-exist, to the benefit of one another, educated and confident in working to towards the natural peaceful progression and growth of the society as a whole.

Quote:

Virtuous people often revenge themselves for the constraints to which they submit by the boredom which they inspire.

Meaning:

This little quote can be tricky to understand, but it's meaning is actually fairly simple. It means that a virtuous person will often chastise themselves for sounding boring when they are proclaiming the benefits of living a virtuous life. Their aim is to promote such a behaviour, but instead they are frustrated by the disinterest it can create in people.

Quote:

He who acts with a constant view to his own advantage will be much murmured against.

Meaning:

When a person always makes decisions for their own benefit, never thinking of others, then naturally, people will talk about them in less than complimentary manner.

A wise person will make their decisions based upon the principle of putting others first.

Quote:

To know what you know and what you do not know; that is true knowledge.

Meaning:

The easy part is knowing what you know. When you enter a field of study, the knowledge of your elders is there to be found, but if you are not aware of it, then you will not know to find it. As such, your knowledge will be lacking.

It is wise to acknowledge when you do not know something. There is no shame in that. It is also wise to recognise the limitations in your knowledge.

A wise person will use this as their motivation to educate themselves to acquire further understanding, but they will never proclaim to have all knowledge. There is always more to learn.

Quote:

To go beyond is as wrong as to fall short.

Meaning:

A wise person will aim to be accurate in their results, and exact in their work.

With people, doing too much or too little for them does not benefit them. Getting it just right may be difficult, but is still the correct action and this takes careful judgement. Too much help can leave a person feeling incapable or undermined. Too little help will leave them in need.

For the person who is carrying out the action, doing too little is not virtuous, and will leave you feeling dissatisfied with yourself. Doing too much, will leave you over-stretched and resentful, and less willing to help in the future.

Quote:

If you look into your own heart and you find nothing wrong there, what is there to worry about? What is there to fear?

Meaning:

If you know in your heart that you have done nothing wrong, then you have nothing to worry about.

If you have done your best in any given situation, then you must know to not fear the outcome.

When things do not go to plan, worry and fear are pointless emotions that will not benefit you. You are not to blame if you have been true.

Quote:

The superior man does not, even for the space of a single meal, act contrary to virtue. In moments of haste, he cleaves to it. In seasons of danger, he cleaves to it.

Meaning:

This highlights the importance of practicing virtue above all else. Even when he is hungry, or late, or in fear of his life, a wise person will still lead a virtuous life, still working towards the benefit of others before themselves.

The more difficult his situation, the stronger his resolve is to act in a virtuous manner.

Quote:

The will to win, the desire to succeed, the urge to reach your full potential; these are the keys that will unlock the door to personal excellence.

Meaning:

These are values that you should use as your motivation in any task.

A wise person will flourish in the competition, the need to achieve and the personal growth. When you embrace these values, you have all you need to follow the true path towards being everything you can be.

Quote:

Go before the people with your example and be laborious in their affairs.

Meaning:

When you are asked for knowledge, you should show them. Give them the benefit of your experience, and then help them as much as you would help yourself.

A good leader will lead by the example of their own deeds, and do their best for the benefit of their people.

Quote:

If we don't know life, how can we know death?

Meaning:

There are two interpretations to this. One is, that a wise person will seek to live a full life. A life that is not fulfilled to its greatest potential, does not display such a great distance or dissimilarity from death.

The second is that if you know much of death, then you will value life and all its possibilities. Conversely, if you know the value of life, then you will come to understand death.

Quote:

The expectations of life depend upon diligence. The mechanic that would perfect his work must first sharpen his tools.

Meaning:

For your expectations of success in life to manifest, you must work hard to prepare, learn, apply knowledge and pay attention to detail.

Preparation before all things is key. As with the 'mechanic who must sharpen his tools', you must hone your knowledge and skills in order to achieve your best outcome.

Quote:

You cannot open a book without learning something.

Meaning:

This quote has a couple of interpretations. If you open a book, pay attention to its contents. Understand its meaning, and from there, you will learn. Education, as a previous quote has already suggested, brings forth knowledge, confidence, hope, and peace. The importance of studying is an essential part of living a virtuous life.

Also, whatever you happen to read, whether it be a book, or, relevant to our times, an email, web page, ebook, etc, there is always some piece of information that we will inevitably learn from, however small. This is inevitable.

Quote:

A gentleman would be ashamed should his deeds not match his words.

Meaning:

A virtuous person will always say as he does and do as he says. It is shameful to claim to have done more than is true and it would lead to distrust among others.

Similarly, he must be honest about his actions, and not tell untruths.

Honesty underpins trust among people within a society.

Quote:

When a person should be spoken with, and you don't speak with them, you lose them. When a person shouldn't be spoken with and you speak with them, you waste your breath. The wise do not lose people. Nor do they waste their breath.

Meaning:

There are several interpretations to this. When a person needs to talk about something that is important to them, you should be there for them to listen and speak with, or you risk losing them as a friend.

Also, when a person needs direction, such as a student, or employee, you should seek to help them. Your help will be remembered by them and you will never lose their respect.

If a person has wronged you, it is not worth wasting your breath speaking with them. Better to walk away.

Also, if a person refuses to listen to you, then again, do not expend energy insisting that they do.

Quote:

To see and listen to the wicked is already the beginning of wickedness.

Meaning:

If you recognise someone or group of people are doing or planning something that you know is wrong, then you should not pay it any of your attention.

You should distance yourself from it. If you listen to what they say, then you are allowing yourself to become a part of that wrong doing.

Quote:

It is more shameful to distrust our friends than to be deceived by them.

Meaning:

If a friend deceives you in some way, you are in no way responsible for that, and therefore hold no blame and have nothing to be ashamed of.

However, if you assume without proof, that your friend is up to no good, then that is shameful. It is not for you to make unwarranted judgement. And you could be wrong. If you distrust an honest friend, you will lose them.

Quote:

By three methods we may learn wisdom. First, by reflection, which is noblest. Second, by imitation, which is easiest. Third, by experience, which is the bitterest.

Meaning:

Wisdom is a quality that must be acquired through learning. The three methods of learning each have their own values.

To learn wisdom by reflection, especially of the self, is the noblest. It is the acknowledgement of one's own weaknesses and strengths and the understanding of how change in oneself could improve an outcome. It is also the reflection of past situations and interactions, and how doing something differently may have altered the result.

To learn wisdom by imitation, as the quote says, is easy. When you recognise a wise decision or action in another, apply those qualities to your own thoughts and plans.

Learning by experience can often be the bitterest way of learning. It suggests that you will learn by your mistakes and failures of the past. But if you gain wisdom from the experience, while it may be bitter, it will still be beneficial.

To learn wisdom, we must embrace all three methods, for all are perfectly valid, essential forms of learning.

Quote:

Wisdom, compassion and courage are the three universally recognised moral qualities of men.

Meaning:

For a person to be deemed virtuous, they must possess all three qualities, as stated in the quote.

Wisdom, to have understanding and knowledge.

Compassion, to be kind and supportive of others.

Courage, to be fearless in all efforts.

This is true in every culture.

Quote:

The more man meditates on good thoughts, the better will be his world and the world at large.

Meaning:

Positive thoughts generate positive emotions. A wise person will feel happier in themselves when focusing on the good.

Similarly, good thoughts will lead to good actions, benefitting others.

Quote:

If you don't want to do something, don't impose on others.

Meaning:

If there was a deed to be done and you do not want to do it, it would be wrong to expect someone else to do it instead.

Furthermore, to impose, suggests that you are forcibly insisting that someone else complete the task which is most certainly wrong.

Quote:

It is easy to hate and it is difficult to love. This is how the whole scheme of things works.

Meaning:

Hate is an easy emotion to fall into. It's a trap that has no good attached to it.

To love is sometimes much harder, especially when it is applied to someone that has wronged you.

It is virtuous to always practice love towards your fellow humans, regardless of their differences or past demeaners.

Quote:

The strength of a nation derives from the integrity of the home.

Meaning:

At a macro scale, this teaches that the integrity of leaders and solidarity of people supplies the strength of the nation.

On a micro scale, this is also true of the family home. The family unit is stronger when they support each other and act with honesty.

Quote:

Never give a sword to a man who can't dance.

Meaning:

This means, most literally, that a person must learn how to use a tool before performing the action of using it.

Similarly, a person must acquire the knowledge and understanding of any action they plan before partaking in that action.

And no-one should ask more of a person than they are capable of achieving.

Overall, this quote tells us that acquisition of knowledge, skill and practice is essential for a successful outcome, but attempting an outcome without sufficient knowledge, skill or practice can be dangerous.

Quote:

We should feel sorrow, but not sink under its oppression.

Meaning:

Sorrow, anguish and emotional pain are genuine human reactions that have their appropriate place and time in our lives.

But if we dwell on these emotions, then we risk falling deeper into a depression that can be hard to climb back up from.

Quote:

Imagination is more important than knowledge.

Meaning:

To be able to imagine, is to be creative and able to think laterally.

This is not to diminish the importance of knowledge, but knowledge to someone with no imagination is very linear, and risks missing potential opportunities for ideas, for invention, for discovery, and for alternative paths for progression.

Knowledge has defined boundaries, but imagination is limitless. Even in oppressive times, when knowledge is withheld or subdued, imagination is left free to roam. It can be the engine for revolution and evolution and as such, is therefore significantly more important than knowledge.

Above: Confucius (551 – 479 BC)

End

If you enjoyed this book, you may also like:

Quotes of Mahatma Gandhi, A Words of Wisdom Collection Book

And more from the Words of Wisdom Collection Book Series

Printed in Great Britain
by Amazon